D1536014

AMAZING EYE TRICKS

AMAZING
EYE TRICKS
-YOU WON'T BELIEVE YOUR EYES-

Gary W. Priester and Gene Levine

ARCTURUS

ARCTURUS

This edition published in 2016 by Arcturus Holdings Limited
26/27 Bickels Yard, 151–153 Bermondsey Street,
London SE1 3HA

ISBN: 978-1-78428-387-2
AD000044EN

Printed in China

Contents

How to view stereograms

This is intended as a guide for viewers who have never seen stereogram 3D effects, and for those viewers who are a bit rusty. Please don't be discouraged if you can't visualize the effects right away. After all, what you are doing is overcoming a lifetime habit of viewing everything with 'normal' stereovision: that which gives us a sense of depth in our everyday viewing of the world.

First, let's try using a physical aid. After that are some practices for viewing autostereograms (stereograms that work without physical aids).

To view hidden-image and stereo-field stereograms, you cannot use normal, or cross-eyed vision (see fig. 1). Instead, you have to use parallel vision, which is what you will do automatically if you place a piece of card between your eyes when viewing the images (see fig. 2).

Unlike cross-eyed vision, there is no strain or discomfort with parallel vision. The essential key, in fact, is to relax your eyes into viewing this way.

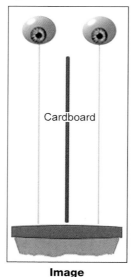

fig. 1 **Normal vision**   fig. 2 **Parallel vision**

Cardboard

Image   Image

Top view

Below is a stereo-pair image. Place the card directly in the middle of the pair, as illustrated in fig. 2. Now move your head to position the other end of the card between your eyes. Disregard focusing for now.

A stereo-pair

If the alignment is good, you should see only one image. Now relax your eyes, and slowly bring things into focus, pulling your head back. Remember, you should not think you see a 3D effect; you should know for sure. When you are sure, hold that focus and remove the card. You should now see three images: the one in the middle containing the 3D effects.

Congratulations, you are now viewing a stereogram as it should be seen!

Continue with the practices without aids, opposite. The only thing you'll need here is two eyes. Let go of the normal way you focus on something on a page. Let your eyes relax.

Viewing practice for autostereograms

Practice 1

The objective here is to let your mind process these two objects until they appear as three. Let your eyes relax, and move your head forward or away until three zeros appear clearly.

Your primary inclination is to focus on the above two objects in the normal way. But now, look behind them; look behind the page and forget about focusing. Try this for a while until you gradually see the three zeros.

When you see a non-existent object appear between the two existing ones, you have mastered the basis of the stereo-pair. It is in the centre object where the 3D effect takes place. This is the crux of autostereograms.

So where does the centre image come from?

It is helpful to remember that visual perception happens in the brain, not the eyes. What we're doing here is fooling the brain. The eyes are feeding it visual information, but not in the usual manner, and so the mind gives us a middle object. And if you introduce some subtle offsets and distortions into two otherwise similar images, the mind will perceive depth even though it is not truly there.

If you view three objects as an autostereogram, you should perceive four objects. Four objects will look as if they are five, and so on.

Practice 2

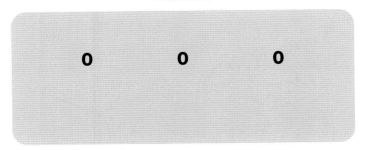

And now for some 3D:

Between these two objects, another object should appear with the smaller square floating over the larger.

Practice 3

Still can't see it?

Pull back, and focus normally on the centre object of the three below. Now lean slowly forward into the page, holding that focus until it is broken or you see four objects, clearly.

Master these practices, and you should have no problem moving on to fully-fledged autostereograms.

Practice 4

© 2003 GENE LEVINE

© 2003 GENE LEVINE

Blue Butterfly

© 2003 GENE LEVINE

© 2002 GEN

© 2003 GENE LEVINE

Colour Sieve

Molten Water

© 2003 GENE LEVINE

© 2004   GENE LEVINE

© 2003 GENE LEVINE

Fireworks

Footprints

© 2004 GENE LEVINE

© 2004 GENE LEVINE

© 2001 GENE LEVINE

© 2003 GENE LEVINE

© 2003 GENE LEVIN

Terraced

© 2004 GENE LEV

Celtic Knot

Dos Espirales

Hello

Indented Cubes

Lock & Key

© 2002 GENE LEVI

© 2000 GENE LEVINE

Pyramid Valley

© 2003 GENE LEVINE

© 2002 GENE LEV

© 2001 GENE LEVINE

© 2003 GENE LEV

Sunflower

Pluses

© 2004 GENE LEVINE

Organic Vacuum

© 2004 GENE

© 2003 GENE LEVINE

view this way

© 2002 GENE LEVINE

view this way

London Disconnect

view this way

124

view this way

view this way

view this way

© 2004

Crown Thee

© 2004 GENE LEVINE

Revelations

page 8   Byzantine Crystal

page 9   Edge of the Woods

page 10   Rose Rows

page 11   Scorpions

page 12   Four Hundred 50 Yen

page 13   Straight as an Arrow

Revelations

page 14   Blue Butterfly

page 15   Butterfly Lines

page 16   Diamonds in the Rough

page 17   Dragonfly Sparks

page 18   Johnny's Garden

page 19   Frax Bubbles

Revelations

page 20   Butterfly Pillows

page 21   Cloud Funnels

page 22   Colour Sieve

page 23   Dragon Light

page 24   Molten Water

page 25   Mixed Vegetables

page 26   Star Screen

page 27   Star Family

page 28   Man & Woman

page 29   Making Honey

page 30   Hidden Image

page 31   GO

Revelations

page 32   Fireworks

page 33   Floral Twists

page 34   Footprints

page 35   Escargot

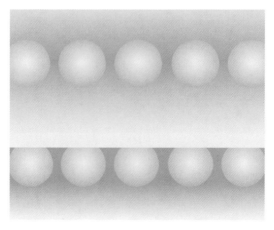

page 36   Gold Eye Sky

page 37   Goldfish

Revelations

page 38   Stone Burst

page 39   The Phrenologist

page 40   Takeoff & Landing

page 41   Temple Albathor

page 42   Heart in Heart

page 43   Heart-throb

Revelations

page 44   Terraced

page 45   The Guardian

page 46   Seahorse Herd

page 47   The Stereogram Machine

page 48   Box in a Box

page 49   Butterfly

page 50   Celtic Knot

page 51   Comedy

page 52   Dice

page 53   Double Spiral

page 54   Dos Espirales

page 55   DNA

Revelations

page 56   Fantasy Nouveau

page 57   Han-nya

page 58   Hello

page 59   Inverted Spheres

page 60   Indented Cubes

page 61   Rings

Revelations

page 62   Lock & Key

page 63   Mystic Shapes

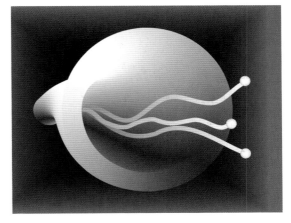

page 64   An Interesting Shape

page 65   Hot-Air Balloon

page 66   Entanglements

page 67   Shamrock

Revelations

page 68 Butterfly Scarf

page 69 Holding Pattern

page 70 Pyramid Valley

page 71 Yang Yin

page 72 Swimming Ocean

page 73 Mermaid

Revelations

page 74   Uproar

page 75   Atmosphere

page 76   Sunset

page 77   End of the Line

page 78   Sea Palace

page 79   River Canopy

Revelations

page 80   Inspiration

page 81   Palais du Lac

page 82   Lotus Garden

page 83   Koa Construction

page 84   Sunflower

page 85   Trilogy 1

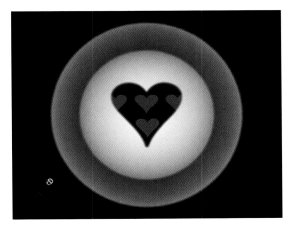

page 86   Hole in My Heart

page 87   Hole in the Desert

page 88   Golden Medley

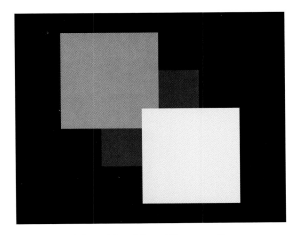

page 89   Floating Cheese Burgers

page 90   Equinox

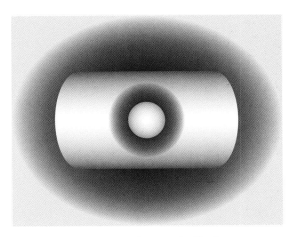

page 91   Grass Cylinder

Revelations

Revelations

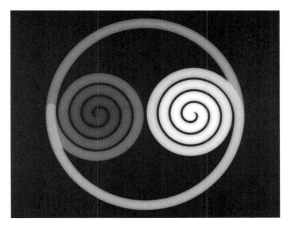

page 98   Spirals – In & Out

page 99   Twisting Star

page 100   Window

page 101   Desert Flower

page 102   Cube & Hoop

page 103   Words

Revelations

page 104   Winter Trees

page 105   Circles

page 106   Cards

page 107   Artemisia Spirals

page 108   Anasazi Petroglyphs

page 109   5 Rings

Revelations

page 110   Organic Vacuum

page 111   Star of David

page 112   Granite Fu

page 113   Jade Riches

page 114   French Chow

page 115   Enbubbled

Revelations

page 116   Sunset on the Nile

page 117   Rising Sun

page 118   Lucky Rabbit

page 119   Mesa Verde

page 120   New Mexico

page 121   Open the Door

Revelations

page 122   Stereo Time

page 123   Aster Turf

page 124   London Disconnect

page 125   Shamrocks

page 126   Blossom Waves

page 127   Fruit Bat

Revelations

page 128   Cherry Blossom

page 129   Crown Thee

page 130   Egyptian Shadows

page 131   Footsteps

page 132   Stereocycle

page 133   Sundial

Revelations

page 134   Wing Wang

page 135   The Yard

page 136   King & Queen

page 137   Head Bands